Wings over LINCOLNSHIRE

Midland Publishing
Limited

© 1994
Peter H T Green, Mike Hodgson,
Bill Taylor and
Midland Publishing Limited

Published by
Midland Publishing Limited
24 The Hollow, Earl Shilton
Leicester, LE9 7NA
England

ISBN 1-85780-024-9

Printed in England by
The Nuffield Press Limited
Cowley, Oxford
OX9 1TR

Designed by
Midland Publishing
and Stephen Thompson Associates

Front cover illustration:
Avro Lancaster PA474 of the Royal Air Force Battle of Britain Memorial Flight, over Burghley House, near Stamford, on 11th September 1979. C F E Smedley

Title page illustration:
A balloon flight is recorded as having taken place at Gainsborough from the Mart Yard on 10th September 1827. It was flown by Charles Green, a well known balloonist and this was his 82nd ascent. The photograph shows a much later ascent made at Gainsborough at the King's Great Gala of 13th July 1874. Mrs E H Rudkin

Introduction illustration - see page 4:
The first aeroplane to be built in Lincoln was the Mackenzie-Osbourne. This was made during 1910 and is seen here on the West Common. It never actually flew, though it reputedly left the ground for a few feet after hitting a bump. James C Ellis

Back cover illustrations, from the top:
Sopwith Camel B7380 - the 1,000th aeroplane to be built by Ruston, Proctor & Co at Lincoln, as it was on 4th January 1918. Ruston, Proctor & Co.

Bristol Beaufort I, L9878 - R of 217 Squadron. This unit was based at North Coates for two months from March 1942. The main Beaufort units based at North Coates were 22, 42 and 86 Squadrons. Charles E Brown

Avro Vulcan K.2, XH560 of 50 Squadron, based at RAF Waddington, photographed on the occasion of the farewell sortie, 14th March 1984. P H T Green

Midland Publishing Limited take considerable pride in the publication of authoritative, quality books that provide long-term value. If you have suggestions for books on aviation, railways and associated subjects that you would like to see published, please write to Midland Publishing at 24 The Hollow, Earl Shilton, Leicester, LE9 7NA.

Wings over
LINCOLNSHIRE

Peter Green · Mike Hodgson · Bill Taylor

INTRODUCTION

No single book about aviation in Lincolnshire could tell the whole story; this one comprises a selection of photographs to fill some of the gaps in previously published material.

The photographs are arranged in five sections: the Early Years, the First World War, Between the Wars, the Second World War and the Later Years. These pictures include balloons, airships, aeroplanes, floatplanes, people and incidents to tell part of the history of aviation in which this county is steeped.

The authors are indebted to many friends and acquaintances for providing photographs over a long period. Unfortunately, in some cases it is now impossible to identify the original photographer and we have quoted the immediate supplier. If we have not correctly credited any photos we apologise.

We are particularly indebted to Lincolnshire County Council and the Museum of Lincolnshire Life who gave us the inspiration for this book, which initially serves as a supplement to the exhibition of the same name which the Museum is staging from 23rd April to 31st July 1994 at its premises in Burton Road, Lincoln. This will be followed by a further three months from early August until 31st October at its outstation, Church Farm Museum, Skegness. Associated with the organising committee of this exhibition, we acknowledge special thanks to Andrew Davies of the Museum and to Bill Baker and Colin Baxter.

We should be most pleased to see any additional photographs of aviation activities in the county, as it is hoped to produce a second volume in due course, to tell more of the county's aviation history.

Finally, we express our gratitude to the team at Midland Publishing Limited in Earl Shilton for producing this book at very short notice.

Peter Green, Mike Hodgson
and Bill Taylor   March 1994

The earliest recorded 'flight' over Lincolnshire was when James Sadler, the first English balloonist, ascended from Birmingham on 7th October 1811. After a distance of some 112 miles he landed near Heckington, close to Sleaford. Sadler was thrown out unhurt, but the balloon continued for another one and a half miles, with the passenger still in the basket, until it hit a tree. The passenger was not hurt either.

There were sundry balloon flights during the nineteenth century, but it was not until 1910 that the first heavier than air machines appeared.

Locally, the Mackenzie-Osbourne machine was built in Lincoln in 1910, but it did not achieve flight. There was no known flying in the county until 1912, when an early local aviator, Mr M F Glew, a farmer's son from South Kelsey, learned to fly at Hendon and soon bought his own aeroplane. This was a Blackburn Monoplane that had been made in Leeds and remarkably this aeroplane survives today in the Shuttleworth Collection at Old Warden, Bedfordshire.

The Royal Navy was looking at landing sites at Skegness and Immingham by 1914: only Immingham was proceeded with. The Royal Flying Corps did little flying in the county prior to the First World War, one notable exception being the transit flight of No.2 Squadron from Montrose in Scotland to Netheravon on Salisbury Plain. This was during May 1914 and the aeroplanes landed near Boothby Graffoe, south of Lincoln.

After the outbreak of war in August 1914 this lack of activity was soon to change.

W H Ewen visited Lincoln in his Caudron biplane on 8th July 1912 when he landed near the Wragby Road, during a tour of Eastern England. He was involved in a slight accident at Peterborough on 1st July which caused some damage but this had been repaired. However, the machine was turned on its back after flying at Lincoln. W Baker collection

Below: Balloon landings were somewhat unpredictable and in many cases, hazardous. This scene was at Barton-on-Humber at a date unknown. Welhome Galleries, Grimsby

Bottom: At about the same time that Ewen was visiting Lincoln, Gustav Hamel was visiting Grimsby, having arrived from Hull. Great crowds turned out to watch him land at Clee Fields, before he took off again and to quote the Grimsby Telegraph of 17th July 1912, 'The machine rushed across the greensward and at the behest of the pilot, rose splendidly'. Peter Pountney

SOUVENIR

EXHIBITION FLIGHTS AT LINCOLN.

ENGRAVED SILVER PLATE

B.C.HUCKS.

PRESENTED TO MR B.C.HUCKS BY LINCOLN ADMIRERS

...BY... MR B.C.HUCKS

COPYRIGHT PHOTO & DESIGN

J.SPENCER BALDAY, LINCOLN.

Another of the well known aviators of the time – B C Hucks – visited Lincoln for the first time on 1st August 1912. Our illustration is a reproduction of a souvenir postcard of this visit. W Baker collection

FLYING

WILL TAKE PLACE AT SPALDING,

On FRIDAY and SATURDAY NEXT,

MAY 30th and 31st,

By the WELL-KNOWN AVIATOR, Mr. B. C. HUCKS.

Entrances to Ground, Tower Lane, Cowbit-rd., & Stonegate.

FLIGHTS each day at 3, 4, and 5 o'clock ; and again at 7 o'clock with BOMB DROPPING DISPLAY.

ADMISSION — Each Day, 1/-.

FOR FURTHER PARTICULARS SEE BILLS.

A. L. SEYMOUR,

Hon. Sec. for the Promoters.

B C Hucks came to Lincoln again on 24th January 1913 and by May he was back in the county when he visited Spalding. This illustration shows an advert from the Lincolnshire Free Press of 27th May 1913. Alastair Goodrum collection

This photograph shows Frenchman Monsieur François crashing at Skegness on 12th September 1912. The machine was badly damaged but the aviator was unhurt. It happened when two spectators got in the way as he was taking off 'and in endeavouring to avoid them he lost his balance and crashed'.
P H T Green collection

AEROPLANE FALLNG, SKEGNESS. SEPT. 12. 1912

Ronald Whitehouse visited Lincoln with his Handley Page type E monoplane. He flew from the Nettleham Road area and also the West Common on Friday 27th and Saturday 28th June 1913. W Baker collection

7

Above: **Montague F Glew beside his crashed Blackburn Monoplane at Legsby Road, Market Rasen on 4th July 1913. A South Kelsey farmer's son, he had learned to fly at Hendon.** *Starbuck*

Below: **B C Hucks is seen here with his Bleriot Monoplane at Nettleham Road on 4th April 1914: his third visit to Lincoln. Note the hessian screening in the left background to thwart non-paying sight-seers. The 'cowboys' were from a visiting show.** *W Baker collection*

Above: **This photograph of the Blackburn Monoplane was signed by M F Glew on 24th July 1913 when he was flying at Fulletby near Horncastle. There had obviously been some rapid repairs made after his crash at Market Rasen. This aeroplane survives today with the Shuttleworth Collection at Old Warden in Bedfordshire and is the oldest British-built aeroplane still capable of flight.** *P H T Green collection*

B. C. HUCKS

Above: **What would the Civil Aviation Authority of today say to this? During Huck's visit to Lincoln in April 1914 he flew between the Cathedral towers. It was presumably well planned because it is highly unlikely that there would have been a photographer on top of the main tower by chance.**
W J Taylor collection

Top right: **A very short time after a hop off the ground was news, an Admiralty DFW biplane, No 154, was flown non-stop from Gosport, intending to go to Immingham, on 13th May 1914. Having left at 7.30 am the pilot flew for seven and a half hours against a head-wind and landed beside the railway line just South of Grimsby, where the machine is seen in the photograph.**
Grimsby Public Library

AEROPLANES NEAR WHALE-BONE LANE

Above: **Claude Grahame-White was another of the famous early aviators who made aeroplanes and promoted flying all over England. An exhibition was due to be held at Blankney Hall on 15th April 1914 in aid of local charities. Two machines were involved, a Bleriot monoplane flown by Frenchman Phillipe Marty and a Grahame-White biplane flown by Mr R H Carr. After leaving Hendon early in the morning of 14th April, both pilots lost their way and landed near Grantham. The ground was not as smooth as it looked and the Grahame-White's engine was damaged. Claude Grahame-White travelled by road from London with a spare engine, which was fitted in less than an hour. The Grahame-White with the Bleriot behind it are seen here at Whale Bone Lane, Grantham, following the forced landing.** Museum of Lincolnshire Life

Another historic flight made during May 1914 was No 2 Squadron's move from Montrose in Scotland to Netheravon on Salisbury Plain. Ten machines left on their journey on 11th May, and they are seen here on the beach at Seaton Carew, just south of Hartlepool, on 14th May. They left for the Knavesmire at York the following day. One machine was damaged en route and they all spent a week at York whilst repairs were carried out. On 22nd May the machines reached Boothby Graffoe, south of Lincoln, where a landing strip had been laid out in a 70-acre field below the Hall. They were delayed a further day due to heavy rain, eventually reaching Netheravon on 30th May. P H T Green collection

The Royal Naval Air Service was in residence at Immingham by 1914 and just before the outbreak of war on 4th August, the local establishment comprised four machines - one Bristol TB.8 No 153 (illustrated), a DFW biplane (not numbered) and two Short type S.38 biplanes, Nos 62 and 64. There were four pilots available and there were twelve Hales grenades to be used as offensive weapons.
P H T Green collection

FIRST WORLD WAR

When the First World War broke out in August 1914, Lincolnshire had only one permanent aerodrome – at Immingham on the Humber Bank; part of a rudimentary plan that had been evolved to protect Britain from aerial attack. The task of home defence was allocated to the Royal Naval Air Service, but when Zeppelin raids began in 1915 and Naval aeroplanes failed to stem the hostile airships, home defence squadrons began to be formed by the Royal Flying Corps, and by the end of the year a barrage line of searchlights, anti-aircraft guns and aerodromes had been established throughout the Eastern counties. Home defence squadrons usually operated from three separate flight stations, interspaced by a system of relief landing grounds at convenient intervals throughout the particular squadrons 'territory'. Flight stations were usually equipped with Bessonneau canvas hangars and a few smaller buildings for accommodation, while landing grounds were little more than grass fields with a wooden hut containing a supply of petrol, landing flares and spares.

By the middle of 1916 the need for front line pilots had grown to such an extent that new training airfields began to be built across the County, in particular along the Lincoln Edge. Training airfields tended to be more permanent with stoutly built hangars (known as aeroplane sheds) and living accommodation.

At the end of hostilities in November 1918 Lincolnshire could boast thirty-seven airfields, ranging in size from the small home defence landing grounds, to the training airfields at Cranwell which covered over three thousand acres. In addition to home defence and training airfields, the county was also home to a seaplane base, aircraft acceptance parks, a gunnery school and kite balloon base.

With the end of the war, the RAF, which had been formed by amalgamating the RFC and RNAS on 1st April 1918, was run-down to a peace-time level and Lincolnshire's airfield population was just three sites by 1921.

The early days of 'the Great War' saw a need for more aeroplanes than Britain's tiny aircraft industry could produce. To alleviate this situation engineering firms from around the country were awarded contracts to build aeroplanes under a manufacturer's licence. Ruston, Proctor & Co, well known traction engine producers in Lincoln, signed a contract on 15th January 1915 to build 100 BE.2c aeroplanes, the first of which is seen here nearing completion in the factory. Ruston's was the first Lincoln firm to enter aeroplane production, building over 2,000 aircraft and around 3,000 engines before production ceased at the end of the war. Ruston, Proctor & Co

Early in 1915 the Lincoln engineering firm of Robey & Co became the second in Lincoln to receive a contract to build aeroplanes – thirty Sopwith type 806 Gun Bus machines. Only seventeen were built as complete aircraft, the remainder being delivered as spares. Robey's purchased a suitable field at Bracebridge Heath to enable their products to be test-flown, the aircraft being transported by road from the Canwick Road works for erection and testing, as evidenced by this photograph of Nos 3849 and 3850.
Museum of Lincolnshire Life, ref D687

Photographs on the opposite page:

Top: **Taken on 1st September 1916, this aerial photograph of the Royal Naval Air Service Central Training Establishment at Cranwell, clearly reveals the amount of construction work that had been carried out since work had begun in December 1915. The hangars of both North (top left) and South (top right) airfields are visible.** *RAF Cranwell*

Bottom left: **On the 19th January 1916, BE.2 No 3999 landed at Cranwell, the first aeroplane to arrive at the still-to-be-completed RNAS Central Training Establishment, part** of HMS Daedalus. **Officially opened on 1st April 1916, Cranwell had become the largest airfield in Britain by 1918, covering over 3,000 acres.** *RAF Cranwell*

Bottom right: **Avro 504C No 1471 was one of the early arrivals at Cranwell, being taken on charge on 8th February 1916. On 16th July of that same year, it was wrecked in a forced landing, during the course of which, although it managed to avoid a line of railway wagons it ended up in the foundations of one of the new buildings under construction.** *RAF Cranwell*

Photograph on this page:

Above: **With the cladding to be completed on one of the large Airship Shed wind screens, work on the Lighter Than Air Section was almost complete by the 21st April 1917. Of the three buildings, the Rigid Shed was the largest, measuring 700ft long by 150ft wide and 100ft high. The middle shed was designed to house Coastal Patrol airships while the third, used for Submarine Scouts, had been moved to Cranwell from Anglesey and had been damaged in a gale in March 1916 while being erected at its new home.** *RAF Cranwell*

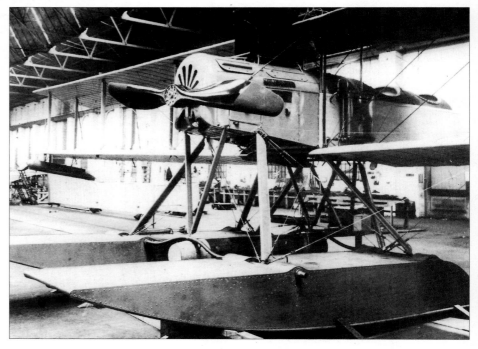

Above left: **Of the three Lincoln firms involved in aircraft manufacture in the First World War, only Robey & Company set about the design and construction of its own aeroplanes. Following its contract for Sopwith Gun Buses in 1915, the company opened a design office under the direction of Mr J A Peters. Two single-seaters were worked on in 1915 but neither reached fruition. Work had started in February 1916 on designing a machine for anti-Zeppelin patrols and in April the Admiralty awarded the company a contract to build two aircraft. Peter's design was for a large biplane with a crew of three; a pilot positioned well back in the fuselage and two gunners in nacelles in the top wing, one to be equipped with a Davis recoil-less gun, the other a Lewis gun. By September 1916 the first machine was ready for testing at Bracebridge Heath and although the first flight was successful, the aircraft overturned on landing following a second circuit of the aerodrome, and was damaged as a result. Disaster overtook the third flight when the machine caught fire and dived into the roof of the nearby St. John's Mental Hospital. Following this incident the Admiralty cancelled its contract but the company continued to build the second aircraft, incorporating many design improvements. However, success again eluded the venture when, on 8th April 1917, the machine stalled on its maiden flight and was destroyed in the ensuing crash. Shortly afterwards Robey closed its design office and Peters left the company.**
Robey & Company

Above: **No 9041 was the first Short 184 float-plane constructed from an order for twenty machines placed with Robey & Co in January 1916. Robey's received a further seven contracts to build over 200 184s. No 9041 was delivered to the flying-boat station at Dundee on 12th June 1916 – by rail. The aircraft was wrecked as a result of an accident on the ground on 23rd August 1916.** *Robey & Co*

Top right: **A Bristol F2b Fighter under construction in the Marshall Sons & Co factory at Gainsborough. The Company was awarded a contract to build 150 aeroplanes in November 1917. Marshalls are believed to have completed the initial contract, but a second contract for a further 100 machines was cancelled when the war ended.** *P H T Green collection*

Above: **Two officers from 83 Squadron, Captain Savery and Lieutenant Colin, photographed at Tydd St Mary early in 1918. At that time 83 Squadron was at Narborough preparing for service on the Western Front. Tydd St Mary was the home of B Flight of 51 Squadron, a Home Defence Unit.** *P H T Green collection.*

Above right: **If the group of photographs to the right are anything to go by, this 1917 pattern aeroplane shed – better known as a Belfast Truss hangar – used by the aeroplane repair section at South Carlton, was a most important place.** *P H T Green collection*

Right: **A souvenir collection dated 1917, which reputedly shows one week's crashes at the Training Aerodrome at South Carlton, north of Lincoln.** *P H T Green collection*

*Above: **A pre-Christmas covering of snow highlights the hangars of the training aerodrome at Waddington, in this fine air-to-air study of a SSZ non-rigid airship taken on ⁺ʰ December 1917.** RAF Waddington*

*Opposite page bottom: **By 6th February 1918, when this photograph was taken, Scampton had become a well established training aerodrome. Opened in 1916 as a Home Defence Flight Station, it was soon developed** as the base for a number of Training Squadrons. At the end of the war the bustling aerodrome, depicted here, was cleared away and returned to the plough.* RAF Scampton*

Above: The pilots of B Flight, 33 (Home Defence) Squadron in the Flight's operations room at Manton (Kirton in Lindsey) in late 1917. The Squadron had arrived in Lincolnshire at the end of 1916 for anti-Zeppelin duties and had established A, B and C Flights at Scampton, Manton and Elsham respectively. The three flights concentrated to Manton in June 1918 and with the diminished threat of Zeppelin attack, finished the war as a night training unit. W J Taylor collection

Above: Avro 504 Night Fighters of 33 Squadron at Manton (Kirton in Lindsey) at the end of the war. Avro 504s replaced the earlier FE.2 and Bristol Fighter aircraft in August 1918 and were only ever used for training purposes. Note the Holt flares just visible under the lower wing tips. P H T Green collection

Opposite page, top: **Clayton & Shuttleworth,**
the third major Lincoln manufacturer to be
involved in aircraft production during the
First World War, had been producing
Sopwith aircraft since early 1916, when it
received a contract to build fifty Handley
Page O/400 bombers on 4th October 1917.
Forty-six were actually constructed, the
majority flying from the Handley Page field,
adjacent to the factory on the outskirts of the
city, to No 4 Acceptance Park, on the West
Common, where two large canvas hangars
were erected to house the aircraft. By the end
of the war, Lincoln had become the largest
centre of aircraft construction in Britain.
Clayton & Shuttleworth & Co

Opposite page, bottom: **A Ruston Proctor &**
Company-built Sopwith Camel fuselage is
hauled through the streets of Lincoln by a
group of 'munitionettes' (women engaged on
war work in the Ruston factories) as part of a
recruiting drive in 1918. *Bill Ward via NKDC*

Above: **Members of the American 11th Aero Service Squadron pose with Bristol Scout C3051 at**
Waddington. American airmen began to arrive at Waddington late in 1917 for additional
training before posting to the Western Front. Scout 3051 was constructed for the RNAS and had
arrived at Cranwell early in 1917. On 5th December 1917 it force-landed near the Rauceby Gun
Station without injury to the pilot. It was repaired and was still at Cranwell on 1st April 1918,
moving to Waddington for the last few months of the war. *P H T Green collection*

Right: **Australian Flying Corps personnel of**
68 Squadron surround de Havilland DH.5
A9197 at Harlaxton. The Squadron formed at
Harlaxton in January 1917 and after working
up was posted to France as a fighter squadron
in the September of that year. A9197 was
named 'New South Wales No.15 – The Upper
Hunter', on 14th April 1917, and was one of
over fifty aeroplanes purchased by public
subscription in Australia during the war.
Colin Baxter collection

The non-rigid airship N.S.11 (NS – North Sea) being walked from its shed at the Lighter Than Air Section, Cranwell. The airship had been delivered in September 1918 and had a brief but eventful career. Shortly after the Armistice it made the first airship flight from Scotland to Norway, and in February 1919 had achieved a world record by staying aloft for 100 hours and 50 minutes. Sadly, while travelling along the North Norfolk coast on 19th July 1919, she was struck by lightning, exploded and crashed into the sea with the loss of all ten of her crew.
P H T Green collection

An SSZ (Submarine Scout Zero) non-rigid airship, with American markings on the ventral fin, flying over the De Aston School, Market Rasen. Two SSZ's were transferred to the US Naval Air Service and used for training purposes with the Lighter Than Air Section, Cranwell, in 1918. Mrs Barraclough

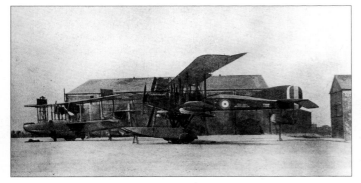

Above: *The Short 320 floatplane, so named because of its 320hp Sunbeam engine, seen here at RNAS Killingholme, first appeared in 1916 in answer to a design requirement for a long range floatplane capable of carrying an 18 inch torpedo. It seems unlikely that any of the few aircraft of the type constructed ever launched a torpedo in anger, even though trials with dummy weapons proved successful, and the aircraft was still operational at the end of the War. MAP*

Below: *This bleak tented camp was provided for the US Naval Air Service personnel who arrived at Killingholme from early in 1918 to assist with North Sea Patrol work. In the background is the huge hangar constructed in 1916 to house the increasing number of flying-boats at the station. 800 feet long and 220 feet wide it was the largest hanger ever to be built in the country and after the war part of it was moved to Grimsby where it is still in use as the town bus depot. P H T Collection*

Above right: *A Curtiss flying-boat being man-handled onto one of Killingholme's two slipways. Using Curtiss H-16 flying-boats, the Americans flew convoy escort patrols and the occasional anti-Zeppelin sorties from Killingholme until the end of the war, completing almost a thousand flying hours for the loss of only two crews. The Americans returned the station to RAF control in January 1919 when the last elements returned to the United States. P H T Green collection*

BETWEEN THE WARS

The end of the War in November 1918 saw a rapid run down in Lincolnshire of the flying being carried out and also of the production of aeroplanes at Lincoln and Gainsborough, where contracts were cancelled at all factories.

A small number of ex-Royal Air Force pilots persevered with joy-riding during the 1920s and 1930s by giving 5/- (25p) flights. They travelled around the country staying one or two days in each place during the summer months. These pilots led a nomadic existance, but as a result many people had their introduction to flying in this way.

The Royal Air Force contracted from the thirty-seven aerodromes it occupied in 1918 to only three by 1925; these were at Cranwell, Digby and Spitalgate/Grantham. By this time flying was at a very low ebb.

In 1929 Sir Alan Cobham toured the length and breadth of Britain to visit civic authorities to try and stimulate an interest in flying. He was successful in a small number of places, and he formed his flying circus in 1932 which toured Britain each summer for the next four years – again, to arouse interest in flying.

Having contracted to a dangerously small size by 1928, the Royal Air Force began to expand very slowly. This expansion increased in tempo after Hitler's rise to power in 1933, but it was still woefully inadequate at the time of the Munich Crisis in September 1938. The extra year until the war started in September 1939 did allow more airfields to be built and newer types of aircraft to come into service.

*Right: **War surplus aeroplanes were available in vast quantities and at a low price after the Armistice had been signed in November 1918. Here an ex-RAF DH.6 biplane is seen on the beach at Cleethorpes giving 'joy-rides' on 14th August 1922. The aircraft was operated by Captain Martin.** W Baker collection*

Martin Aviation Co. Aerial Joy-Rides.

*Below: **One of the few RAF airfields to remain active was Spitalgate near Grantham. In this photograph, from left to right, are an Avro Aldershot of 99 Squadron, a Vickers Vimy, a Vickers Virginia III, and a DH.9A of 39 Squadron based at Spitalgate. The photograph is dated 1924.** Wing Commander Hollingsworth*

Above: 39 Squadron was based at Spitalgate from 12th March 1921 to 12th January 1928. The unit was equipped with the DH.9A for the whole of this time. MoD, H1511

Right: Joy-riding continued to be popular during the 1920s and 1930s. A widely used type was the Avro 504K, hundreds of which had been built during the war as trainers. Many toured the length and breadth of Britain giving five-bob (5/- or 25p) flips. This particular one, G-EASG of Southern Counties Aviation Co, is seen at Harlaxton, near Grantham in the early 1920s. Colin Baxter

Left: **North Coates Fitties near Grimsby was in use during the First World War but was closed down by the end of 1919 and returned to agriculture. By late 1926 it was again being leased for use as an Armament Practice Camp for the RAF, and this oblique view looking north shows the tented accommodation in use during the summer of 1927. It was a bleak site situated right on the North Sea coast.** *P H T Green collection*

Below left: **In 1927 the Royal Air Force Reserve Squadrons were formed and No 503 (County of Lincoln) Squadron was based at Waddington. The first four reserve officers are seen here in May 1927; they are, from left to right, T H Worth, D G Allison, N D Wardrop and R Maw. Roger Maw went on to have a distinguished career in the RAF. He commanded 12 Squadron, equipped with Wellingtons at Binbrook until October 1941, then he went out to North Africa to become Commanding Officer of 108 Squadron, another Wellington unit, but in the process of re-equipping with Liberators. He was shot down in August 1942, taken prisoner of war and sent to Stalag Luft III where** he designed and helped to build the famous wooden vaulting horse used to make one of the most daring PoW escapes. *RAF Waddington*

Below right: **Royal Air Force flying-boats carried out coastal cruises from time to time, around the coast of Britain. One of these was made during the summer of 1927 when the five Supermarine Southamptons of 480 Flight flew from Scarborough to Skegness on 16th September. A Southampton is seen here flying past Skegness pier. After mooring on the beach the machines took off later in the day and were flown across the Wash to Hunstanton.** *P H T Green collection*

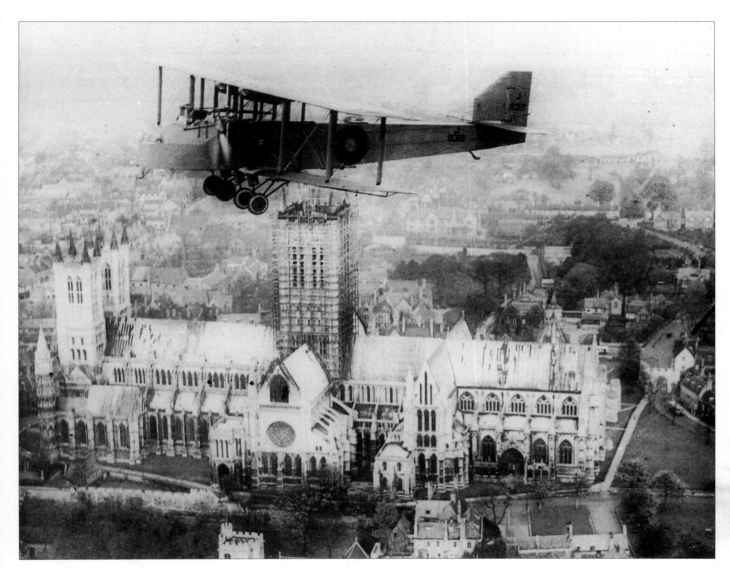

After being initially equipped with Fairey Fawns in October 1926, 503 Squadron started to re-equip with Handley Page Hyderabads in February 1929. One of these – J8321 – is seen here flying over Lincoln Cathedral on 25th October 1931. The Hyderabads were replaced by Handley Page Hinaidis in 1933 and these were in use until replaced by Westland Wallaces in 1935. The latter were only in service with the unit for one year and Hawker Harts arrived in 1936. These were joined by Hawker Hinds which remained in use until the unit disbanded in October 1938.
RAF Waddington

Left: During 1929 Sir Alan Cobham made a tour of towns and cities in Britain to arouse interest in aviation, taking aloft many civic dignitaries and a great many school children. His DH.61 Giant Moth, G-AAEV, is seen here at Toot Hill, Grimsby on 1st October, with Sir Alan being greeted by the Mayor of Grimsby, Councillor Malcolm Smith (centre). Also see opposite page, bottom right. Frank Smith

Centre left: Long distance flights were a feature of the 1930s. Cranwell was the starting point for several of these because it had one of the longest take-off areas available at the time. After the loss of the first Fairey Long Range Monoplane in the Altas Mountains in an earlier attempt, the second machine, K1991, seen here, successfully broke the World's long distance record by flying from Cranwell to Walvis Bay in South West Africa This was a distance of 5410 miles, making a great circle distance of 5341 miles (8597 km). The aircraft, piloted by Squadron Leader O R Gayford and navigated by Flight Lieutenant G E Nicholetts left Cranwell on 6th February 1933 and arrived in South West Africa 57 hours 25 minutes later. Flight, 11286

Bottom left: German Zeppelins visited Lincolnshire several times during the First World War, but this is the Graf Zeppelin flying past Cleethorpes promenade on 19th August 1931. Later visits by Graf Zeppelin II and the Hindenburg overflew many strategic areas, just prior to the Second World War. Grimsby Public Library

Below: The aerodrome at Winthorpe, Skegness was one of the earliest civil aerodromes in Lincolnshire. It was laid out in 1930 next to the Royal Oak public house, on the Roman Bank, by Mr M D L Scott and Captain G A R Pennington who were directors of Eastern Air Transport Limited. The first aircraft were a DH.60G Moth, G-AAKM (illustrated) and a DH.80A Puss Moth, G-AAXL. W J Taylor collection

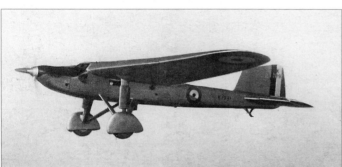

Above: Winthorpe soon became very active following the formation of the Skegness and East Lincolnshire Aero Club. There was a successful opening Air Pageant on 16th May 1932 when some forty aeroplanes arrived. DH.80A Puss Moth G-AAXX is seen on that occasion at the unique petrol pumps with swinging arms that could serve either aircraft or motor traffic on the Roman Bank. P H T Green collection

Right: Sir Alan Cobham continued to promote air mindedness in Britain by setting up a 'Flying Circus' in 1932. This circus toured towns and cities so that the public could see a variety of aeroplanes and also to get a chance to fly. The air days continued for four years until the end of 1935 when the whole organisation was sold to C W A Scott. Part of the Cobham fleet is seen here flying over Burton Road in Lincoln on 7th June 1933; the aircraft are Avro 504K G-ACCX, DH.60G Moth G-ABUL, Handley Page W.10 G-EBMM, DH.83 Fox Moth G-ACEY, and another Avro 504K – G-ABVH (see opposite page). Lincolnshire Echo

Another coastal airfield in Lincolnshire was Sutton Bridge (see page 35) which was established on 2nd September 1926 as an Air Armament School. Squadrons arrived for a few weeks at a time to use the ranges on Holbeach Marsh (see page 29). This photograph, taken around 1933/4, shows Hawker Demons, Fairey Gordons and Bristol Bulldogs on the airfield and Cross Keys Bridge, which carried the Midland & Great Northern Joint Railway across the River Nene, can be seen top left. A Richardson via Terry Hancock

Another 'joy-riding' photograph shows Avro 504N G-ADFW, of the Lincolnshire Flying Services, near Mablethorpe in 1934/5. This company was formed by Mr F Wright who operated the Wright Bus Company at Louth. F Wright

Above: Alex Henshaw, one of Lincolnshire's most famous airmen, started to fly on 20th April 1932 in a DH Gipsy Moth. One of his most interesting aeroplanes was the Arrow Active – G-ABIX – which he acquired in 1935, this being the only one of its kind, although there was an Arrow Active II which was similar (see page 31). MAP

*Above right: **Fortunately Alex Henshaw wore a parachute when he flew, and this saved his life when the Arrow Active burst into flames whilst flying inverted and crashed at Covenham on 30th December 1935. He is seen here with the local constable, surveying the wreckage.** P H T Green collection*

*Right: **This is one of the targets on Holbeach Marshes mentioned in the caption for the photograph at the top of the opposite page. The photograph on this page was taken in 1935 during 13 Squadron's practice camp at Sutton Bridge.** P H T Green collection*

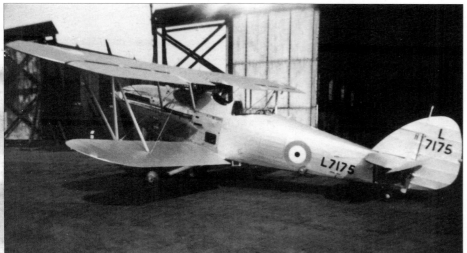

As the RAF expansion programme took effect during the 1930s, 73 Squadron was reformed with Hawker Fury IIs at Mildenhall on 15th March 1937. This unit received Gloster Gladiators as a temporary measure in June 1937, moving to Digby on 9th November where they were photographed early in 1938. They received Hawker Hurricane Is in July 1938. *RAF Cranwell*

The Royal Air Force continued to re-equip and large numbers of Hawker biplanes were built to enable squadrons to be re-established as rapidly as possible. Here we see a Hawker Hind of 211 Squadron at Spitalgate in 1938. No 211 had been reformed on 24th June 1937 at Mildenhall, equipped with Hawker Audax, but was rapidly re-equipped with the Hinds which it used until the Bristol Blenheim Is arrived in April 1939. *Geoffrey Gardiner*

Bottom right: Aerial advertising using either smoke or banners was a feature of the period between the wars. The banners were furled on rollers below the wing, usually on Avro 504Ks or 'Ns. Avro 504N G-ACZC is seen following a forced landing in Kew Gardens, London and is of interest because it was operated by the Aerial Advertising Company, 350 Pelham Road, Immingham, which was the address of a doctor's wife, Mrs MacDougal. She had formed the company with Captain H B Michelmore, who was an instructor with the Lincolnshire Aero Club at Waltham, near Grimsby. The pilot on this occasion was Mr B H Henderson. P H T Green collection

Below: Alex Henshaw had a distinguished career before the war as an air race pilot. He is seen here on 2nd July 1938 in his Percival Mew Gull before the start of the King's Cup Air Race from Hatfield, which he won at a record speed of 236.25 mph. His most memorable flight was the record breaking journey to Cape Town, starting from Gravesend on 5th February 1939, arriving at Cape Town on the 6th. He then started the return flight on the 7th and arrived back at Gravesend on the 9th when he broke the Cape-London record as well as achieving the London-Cape-London record. It was all the more remarkable as it was done by dead reckoning as there were no radio aids in those days. Alex Henshaw went on to become Chief Test Pilot for the Vickers Armstrong factory at Castle Bromwich on 1st June 1940, where he made 33,918 test flights in Spitfires and over 900 test flights in Lancasters, which the factory went on to make (see page 29).
Alex Henshaw

Above: The Electrical and Wireless School was based at Cranwell for many years. This formation of three of the school's aircraft was taken around 1938 and illustrates a Westland Wapiti IIa – K2299, a Vickers Valencia, K8850 and a Westland Wallace II, K6049. A S Thomas

*Left: **This interesting photograph of RAF Waddington was taken in 1939, with the view looking north west and shows the expansion development of that airfield. The new 'C' type hangars are centre rear and some of the surviving First World War hangars are in the foreground (see page 16).** RAF Waddington*

*Bottom left: **Waltham aerodrome situated near Grimsby had been opened as a civil aerodrome in 1933 and the Lincolnshire Aero Club had its base there. In this photograph the club house and club hangar can be seen in the foreground whilst the new Municipal and RAFVR hangars can be seen in the distance. After this photograph was taken in April 1939 the club house was moved to the left of the nearest hangar in the distance and remained there until recently. The aerodrome was further developed in 1941 to become RAF Grimsby.** Grimsby Public Library*

*Below: **One of the first American planes to arrive in Britain before the war was the North American Harvard I, which came into service with 12 FTS at Spitalgate in 1939. Three of their first aircraft (N7004, N7010 and N7005) are seen here flying near Grantham.***

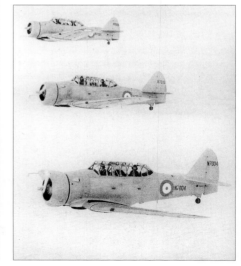

Top right: One of the units based at RAF Waddington in 1939 was 110 Squadron which had reformed there on 13th May 1937. Its initial equipment of Hawker Hinds started to be replaced by the Bristol Blenheim I during January 1938. This example is L1304. MAP

Centre right: As a means of training more pilots after the Munich Crisis in September 1938 the Civil Air Guard was announced. This was a scheme to enable people who wanted to fly but who could not afford to do so, to have subsidised flying lessons at 10/- (50p) per hour with training taken up to the normal 'A' licence standard. Altogether, eighty-three Civil Air Guard members at Waltham qualified for the 'A' licence. The figures centre front row are: Galley (instructor), Darlow (Manager), Michelmore (instructor) - see page 31, and Richmond (instructor). P H T Green collection

Bottom left: Another reformed unit that flew Hawker Hinds as a stop-gap measure, was 49 Squadron which moved from Worthy Down in Wiltshire to Scampton during March 1938, and was the first to re-equip with Handley Page Hampdens. Their first machine, L4039, is seen here shortly after arrival at Scampton in September 1938. RAF Scampton

Bottom right: To close the section, we show 50 Squadron Handley Page Hampden VN:G, on dispersal at Waddington on 3rd September 1939. Together with the Blenheims, the Hampdens, Wellingtons and Whitleys were the mainstay of Bomber Command during the first two years of the war. W Baker

SECOND WORLD WAR

In 1935 while the politicians were talking of peace they were also beginning to prepare for war and a massive expansion programme for the armed forces was put into operation. In Lincolnshire construction work on ten airfields was started and by the time war was declared in September 1939 bombers were already operating from Hemswell, Scampton and Waddington. Airfields built during the expansion period are easily recognised by their stout brick hangars and buildings.

By 1941, when the British counter offensive against industrial Germany was gathering momentum, Lincolnshire's strategic location for bomber airfields was exploited to the full. Out of some three dozen new airfields commissioned during the war the great majority were operational bomber stations. In 1939 even the largest bomber aircraft could take off from all-grass flying fields but as bigger and heavier aircraft entered service and the level of operations increased so a system of hardened runways linked by a taxiway was introduced. Accommodation on wartime 'emergency' airfields was limited to temporary brick, Nissen or wooden buildings and the distinctive black T2 hangar, used for servicing aircraft that usually spent their life parked out at dispersal points around the airfield perimeter.

In addition to the majority of bomber airfields, sites in the County were also used by Coastal, Fighter and Training Commands and by the end of the War Lincolnshire contained forty-nine military airfields, more than any other county in Great Britain.

As soon as the War ended the RAF underwent a massive contraction with virtually all the wartime 'emergency' airfields being closed down, leaving the pre-war expansion sites with their permanent brick hangars and well appointed domestic accommodation to be developed for the peacetime air force.

Hurricane V7434 of 151 Squadron parked in one of RAF Digby's earthen blast pen disposal points. The Squadron had spent the Battle of Britain at North Weald and had come north to Digby to rest and recuperate on the 1st September 1940. DZ-R was the personal mount of Pilot Officer (later Group Captain) I S 'Black' Smith, a New Zealander who volunteered for RAF service in the late 1930s. His Maori 'Tikki' good luck emblem can be seen painted above the fuselage roundel. On the 2nd October 1940, while on a training flight, Smith was vectored onto the tail of a lone Heinkel He111 which he shot down onto the beach at Chapel St. Leonards. Hurricane V7434 was written off in a night flying accident by one of the other Squadron pilots on the 26th October, before the Squadron moved to Bramcote on the 28th November 1940. Group Capt I S Smith

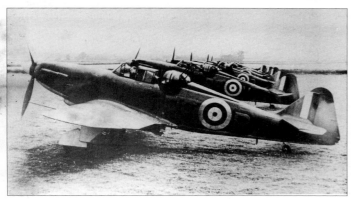

A line up of Boulton Paul Defiant 1 four-gun turret fighters of 264 (Madras Presidency) Squadron at Kirton in Lindsey in early August 1940. The Squadron had been the first unit to equip with the Defiant in December 1939. In 1940 there were some initial successes with the power operated turret over Dunkirk but once the Germans became aware of the lack of forward firepower and were able to indentify Defiants from Hurricanes the Squadron began to suffer too high a loss rate and were redeployed to operate night patrols. However, with the onset of the Battle of Britain, 264 reverted to day operations and on the 23rd August moved south to Hornchurch to take part in the battle. Once again heavy losses – six aircraft on the 24th, three on the 26th and seven on the 28th, resulted in the Squadron being withdrawn to Kirton in Lindsey on the 29th August, where they again commenced night fighter duties. A S Thomas

RAF Sutton Bridge was the home of No 6 Operational Training Unit. When this photograph was taken in the autumn of 1940 it was equipped with a multitude of aircraft including over seventy Hawker Hurricanes. With the threat of imminent invasion, signs of slit trenches and gun positions can be seen around the camouflaged hangars and buildings (see page 28). P H T Green collection

Right: **On the night of 15th September 1940 a force of 155 aircraft of Bomber Command were dispatched for widespread operations over the Channel ports and targets in Germany. No 83 Squadron, based at RAF Scampton, contributed fifteen Hampdens to this force with the invasion barges being assembled in Antwerp docks as their target. Over the target one of the Squadron's aircraft, piloted by Pilot Officer C A Connor, a Canadian volunteer with the RAF, was hit by cannon fire and set alight. Two of the crew baled out leaving Sgt John Hannah, the 18-year-old wireless operator/air gunner, to extinguish the blazing radio compartment (pictured here) – initially with extinguishers and then his log book and bare hands – and to assist Connor to fly the damaged aircraft safely to base. For his brave deeds Hannah was awarded Britain's highest award for gallantry – the Victoria Cross, one of eight Bomber Command VCs awarded to air crew flying from Lincolnshire during the Second World War. He was the youngest member of the RAF to earn the award.** *83 Squadron Records*

Right: **Sgt John Hannah convalescing from the injuries received extinguishing his burning aircraft on the night of the 15th September is pictured here (centre) with one of his nurses and fellow patients at RAF Hospital Rauceby. Hannah never fully recovered and was discharged from the RAF in December 1942.** *83 Squadron Records*

The sad remains of Handley Page Hampden AD983 on Greestone Stairs in Lincoln on the morning of 27th July 1941. The aircraft, from 44 Squadron based at RAF Waddington, had been returning from a mine-laying operation around the Frisian Islands when it got into difficulties and crashed into Lindum High School. In addition to the four man crew, one of the school's teachers, Miss Edith Fowle, was also killed. Lincolnshire Echo

A Fairey Battle of 142 Squadron flies over the snow covered Lincolnshire Wolds in the Winter of 1940/41. Following the fall of France, 142 Squadron – part of the Advanced Air Striking Force – brought its surviving Battles to Binbrook where they continued to be operated until replaced by Vickers Wellingtons early in 1941. A D Gosman

Above: **12 Squadron began to convert from Fairey Battles to Vickers Wellingtons at Binbrook at the end of 1940, moving to Wickenby, a satellite airfield to Binbrook, at the end of September 1942. Wellington II W5424, pictured here, joined the Squadron from 158 Squadron, only to crash on take off at Binbrook on 29th July 1942.**
P H T Green collection

Right: **Britains first ever jet flight was made from RAF Cranwell's runway on the evening of 15th May 1941. In the gathering dusk the little Gloster E28/39, powered by the Whittle W-1 turbojet and unofficially named 'Pioneer' made a successful 15-minute flight. Without an official camera crew present, the only record of this occasion is this blurred shot taken by one of the small party there to witness this important event.** *N Daunt*

Above: **207 Squadron reformed at RAF Waddington on 1st November 1940 as the first Bomber Command unit to operate the new twin-engined Avro Manchester heavy bomber. The aircraft's Rolls-Royce Vulture engines were less than successful and only seven front line Squadrons were equipped with the Manchester, all of them suffering groundings and cancelled operations due to engine problems. Unlike many of its type, L7513, seen here, survived service with 207, 106 and 49 Squadrons and 1650 Conversion Unit before being scrapped in 1943.** *MAP*

Below left: **The scene in front of No 2 hangar at RAF Swinderby on 16th August 1941, when the Polish Air Force Colour was handed over to General Stanislow Ujejski, C-in-C Polish Air Force, by General Wladyslaw Sikorski, C-in-C Polish forces and Prime Minister of Poland. The silken Colour had been made in secret in Wilno in 1940 – while the town was under Soviet occupation – and was smuggled out of Poland by a Japanese diplomat who took it to Sweden, via Berlin, before it was transported to London and eventually Swinderby. Following the presentation, the Colour was handed over to 300 Squadron, the first Polish Air Force Squadron to be formed in Britain, and it was then held by each Polish Squadron in turn on a three-monthly rotation basis. After the war, the Colour was held at the Sikorski Institute in London until the political situation in Poland allowed it to be returned home. In September 1992, Air Vice-Marshal Maisner, President of the Polish Air Force Association and a former Deputy Commandant at Cranwell, handed over the Colour to the C-in-C Polish Air Force in the presence of Lech Walesa, President of Poland. The Colour is now laid up in the church of the Polish Air Force Academy, Deblin.** *P H T Green collection*

Right: The Miles Master two-seat advanced trainer had been designed in 1937 by the Phillips & Powis Company in anticipation of the need for a monoplane training aircraft for the expanding Royal Air Force. Originally powered by a Rolls Royce Kestrel engine, later variants were fitted with radial powerplants, like this Cranwell-based Mk.III which used the American-built Pratt & Whitney Wasp Junior. Over 3,000 Masters gave sterling service throughout the war years. MAP

Below: This Messerschmitt Me (Bf) 109E-4 (W Nr 4869) was exhibited on the forecourt of the Central Station in Lincoln early in November 1940, to encourage fund raising for War Weapons Week. It had been shot down near Tenterden in Kent on Saturday, 12th October 1940 by Flight Lieutenant Stanford Tuck. Lincolnshire Echo

Above: **Throughout the war years Their Majesties King George VI and Queen Elizabeth paid many visits to RAF airfields throughout Britain, visiting Lincolnshire on several occasions. Here on 27th May 1943 they are pictured at RAF North Coates.** *M Hodgson collection*

Above: **On 23rd March 1943, a new Squadron, No 617, began to form at RAF Scampton – tasked with Operation 'Upkeep' – the destruction of the Ruhr Valley dams, using Lancaster aircraft specially modified to carry the Barnes Wallis-designed bouncing bomb. ED817, pictured here, was the second prototype B.III (Special) which was used to test-drop 'Upkeep' weapons at Reculver in Kent, but did not take part in the actual mission. The attack on the dams took place on the night of 16/17th May 1943 with two dams, the Möhne and the Eder being successfully breached. Of the seventeen aircraft that took part in the mission only nine returned to Scampton; fifty-three aircrew had been killed and three became prisoners of war. The leader of the Squadron, Wing Commander Guy P Gibson, was awarded a Victoria Cross, one of thirty-five awards for gallantry made to participants of the attack.** *F G Swanborough collection*

Centre left: **Although not positively identified, this Lancaster seen in the mouth of the Haven near Boston is probably L7570 of 97 Squadron. On 20th March 1942 the Squadron used Lancasters on operations for the first time when six aircraft were ordered from Woodhall Spa to lay sea mines in enemy waters. Flying Officer Rod Rodley took off in L7570 in driving rain at about midday. Holding the aircraft down low and heading out towards the Wash, he broke through the low cloud over Boston, and then had to bank hard to miss St Botolphs Church – the famous Boston Stump – but one wing-tip clipped a house roof while the other turned up at a right angle to the wing. Struggling to control the aircraft, Rodley managed to clear the town and make a successful belly landing on mudflats at Frieston, without injury to his crew. The Lancaster – minus its tailplane but complete with a full load of six mines on board – was recovered during low tide periods by members of 58 MU, which was at that time based at Newark.** *Mrs P Grommett*

Top right: Spitfire Vb W3815 had already seen service with a number of RAF fighter Squadrons when it was transferred to the USAAF. It is seen here in the markings of 555 Training Squadron, part of the 496 Fighter Training Group of the 8th Air Force which was based at Goxhill from December 1943 until the end of the War.
P H T Green collection

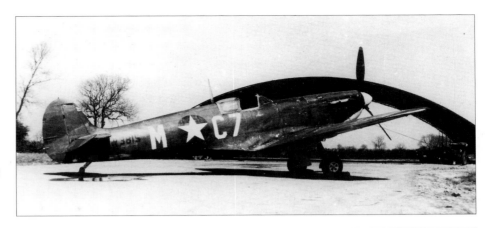

Centre right: Goxhill airfield was opened on 26th June 1941 for 1 Group Bomber Command and was used by No 1 Group Target Towing Flight. This flight departed Goxhill on 10th November 1941 and the airfield was handed over to Fighter Command. However, Americans started to arrive in June 1942 and the airfield became a training base for USAAF fighter pilots. Amongst the types used were Lockheed P-38 Lightnings, Bell P-39 Aira-cobras, and some Spitfires. North American P-51 Mustangs arrived later. Many pilots experienced problems with the P-38; there were several crashes mainly because they were more used to flying single-engined aircraft. The result was that the pilots became frightened of the P-38. In order to overcome this, Tony LeVier – the Lockheed Chief Test Pilot – was sent over to the UK in 1944 to restore pilot confidence. He gave them a startling display in his own aircraft and after much scepticism he picked out a unit aircraft at random and proceeded to do the same again. His P-38, named 'Snafuperman' is seen here at Goxhill. The name is derived from the acronym SNAFU – Situation Normal All Fouled Up! *P H T Green collection*

Bottom right: The fuselage of a Short Stirling of 1660 Conversion Unit is lifted onto a trailer by members of 58 MU at Swinderby following a landing accident early in 1944. Note the damage to the bomb bay doors. The aircraft was repaired and later went on to serve with 1332 Conversion Unit before being eventually struck off charge in May 1945.
W J Taylor collection

41

Left: The versatile Bristol Beaufighter, originally designed in 1938 as a high speed long range fighter, equipped the first Coastal Command Strike Wing which formed at North Coates in November 1942. Two Squadrons; 236 (Bomber) and (254 Torpedo), later joined by 143 Squadron with fighter Beaufighters, began to carry out co-ordinated attacks on the enemy convoys bringing vital iron ore cargoes from Scandinavia to the European ports. The Beaufighter X, depicted here, was capable of carrying a torpedo, bombs or rockets – or a combination of the three. This aircraft, NT950, was destined to be hit by flak and abandoned near the Dutch coast during operations on 3rd October 1944. MAP

Centre left: Mosquito B.25 KB416 AZ-P of 627 Squadron at Woodhall Spa in the autumn of 1944. 627 Squadron had been formed with Mosquitos from C Flight of 139 Squadron at RAF Oakington on 12th November 1943, within No 8 Pathfinder Group. In April 1944 the Squadron was transferred to Woodhall Spa to act as a low level visual marker unit to operate with 5 Group bomber squadrons, a task that was carried out until the end of hostilities. Canadian-built KB416 was added to Squadron strength at the end of October 1944 but on 3rd July 1945 the aircraft was destroyed by fire when it stalled and crashed attempting a single-engined landing at RAF Woodhall Spa. The pilot, Flight Lieutenant Johnson was killed and the navigator, Pilot Officer Finlayson, was injured. Corporal Steven Cogger was in charge of the Woodhall Spa fire party on the day of the crash and made repeated attempts to rescue the crew although suffering serious burns. He released the navigator and returned to the blazing aircraft, but was unable to reach the pilot. For this display of gallantry Corporal Cogger was awarded the George Medal, receiving his award on 26th February 1946. Douglas Garton

RAF Metheringham was a typical wartime heavy bomber airfield with its three runway system. Twenty-eight such heavy bomber airfields were constructed in Lincolnshire during the Second World War. Additionally, Metheringham was equipped with FIDO (Fog Identification Dispersal Operation), clearly visible along each side of the main runway in this aerial photograph. Using 1500 gallons of petrol per minute pumped through the system at a pressure of 75lbs per square inch, when ignited, the heat generated was sufficient to disperse the fog allowing aircraft to land with safety. *P H T Green collection*

Opposite page, bottom:
Men of the 1st Parachute Brigade await their turn to take off from Barkston Heath to participate in Operation 'Market Garden', the ill-fated attack on the Rhine bridge at Arnhem. On Sunday 17th September the US 9th Troop Carrier Command provided 157 Dakota aircraft for the operation, using the airfields at Barkston Heath, Folkingham and Fulbeck. *Humberside Aircraft Preservation Society*

One of the dangers to aircrews on bombing missions was the threat of being hit by 'friendly' bombs being released by higher flying aircraft. This 101 Squadron Lancaster was hit by this shower of 500 lb bombs but despite damage was able to make a safe return to its home base at Ludford Magna. *Victor Redfern*

As a result of the problems with Dunholme Lodge's circuit overlapping Scampton's, it was decided to cease operational flying at the former. Late in 1944 a Ministry of Aircraft Production Glider modification team of seventeen men arrived from General Aircraft Limited, to work on the Hamilcar gliders. One of the modifications was to fit two Bristol Mercury engines to enable an empty Hamilcar to take off again and return to base. The Hamilcar X prototype LA728 is shown. *R C B Ashworth*

VE night, 8th May 1945 – Air and Ground crew personnel celebrate the end of the war in Europe outside the NAAFI on No 1 Communal Site at RAF Woodhall Spa. After being completely derelict for many years, this building and others on the site, have been restored and are part of the Thorpe Camp Museum which is due to open in the middle of 1994. *Douglas Garton*

POST WAR

As soon as the Second World War finished, the wartime airfields of Lincolnshire started to be de-activated and closed down. Skellingthorpe and Kelstern were already closed by October 1945 and others followed.

At several airfields where flying ceased, activity continued for some years as storage sites and Ministry dispersal sales were held to dispose of a great deal of surplus equipment.

The Berlin Crisis and the infamous airlift of 1948/9 caused a slow down in the closures, but contraction continued until the time of the Korean War of 1951, which created a modest expansion again.

Some airfields such as East Kirkby, Spilsby and Sturgate were re-activated to provide bases for the United States Air Force which was moving back into Europe because of the continued 'cold war' with Russia.

The mid-'fifties heralded a peak in Bomber Command's post-war strength, with Canberras stationed at Binbrook, Coningsby, Hemswell, Scampton and Waddington. The first Vulcans arrived at Waddington for 230 OCU in August 1956

Further airfields were also bought back into use during the late 'fifties for the deployment of Douglas Thor intermediate range ballistic missiles. Hemswell was selected as one of the Headquarters and used for receiving the missiles from the United States. Bardney, Caistor, Coleby Grange and Ludford Magna were the satellite sites for Hemswell, whilst Folkingham was a satellite site of North Luffenham.

Bloodhound surface-to-air missiles were also based at various stations in the county, with the headquarters at North Coates and other sites at Dunholme Lodge, Barkston Heath and Woodhall Spa.

Binbrook was closed down as a Bomber Command base on 31st December 1959 and was re-allocated to Fighter Command in April 1960. It was not, however, reopened until April 1962 when it housed Javelin fighters for a short time before becoming well known as a Lightning base in 1965.

From the 1960s onwards there has been a steady run-down of the Royal Air Force in Lincolnshire with squadrons disbanding and stations being closed. There are now only four active airfields which see flying taking place – Coningsby, Cranwell, Scampton and Waddington. This is a far cry from the wartime total of forty-five.

Civil flying was slow to recover after the war, but a new airfield was opened at Ingoldmells near Skegness in 1948 to serve Butlin's holiday camp and remained in use until it was closed down in 1993. Most of the other civil flying has been on a small scale, operating from farm strips scattered about the county. Some gliding has taken place at Kirton in Lindsey and other airfields.

Lindsey County Council bought Kirmington airfield in 1970 to develop as a civil airport. This was opened on 26th March 1974 just before the boundary changes took place.

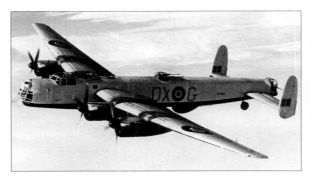

*Right: **Lincoln RF385 was one of the first to be delivered to the RAF, joining 57 Squadron at East Kirkby in 1945. It is in the 'Tiger Force' black and white colour scheme. The aircraft was destined to crash in Leicestershire in February 1946.** MAP*

*Far right: **Whilst 19 Flying Training School was primarily based at Cranwell, a number of its aircraft operated from Digby between 1946 and 1948. Tiger Moth DE454 is seen here at Digby in 1947.** M Hodgson*

*Bottom right: **An immediate post-war photograph of RA597 – a 300 Squadron Lancaster.***

No 300 was the first Polish Squadron to be formed in the UK, in 1940, at Bramcote in Warwickshire. It moved to Swinderby on 22nd August 1940 and following various moves within Lincolnshire, eventually disbanded at Faldingworth in October 1946. It was the only Polish Squadron to fly Lancasters. RA597 went into storage and was struck off charge on 25th March 1948. In the photograph, note the white instead of red Squadron codes as well as the re-instated underwing serial. M Ingham

Above: **Photographed flying above the docks at Grimsby in May 1949 is Lincoln B.2 RF523, which carried the name 'Thor II' whilst operating with the Empire Air Armament School at Manby.**
Grimsby Evening Telegraph

Left: **Approaching to land at Swinderby on 17th May 1948 is Wellington T.10 RP547 of 201 Advanced Flying School.**
P H T Green collection

Right: At the height of the 1948 Berlin crisis, the United States Air Force stationed a large number of Boeing B-29A aircraft in the UK. Scampton was one of the stations selected to house the B-29s, one of which is seen here undergoing a 100-hour inspection.
Brig Gen Brian S Gunderson USAF Retd

*Bottom right: **Just as it did all through the wartime years, the Salvation Army refreshment van provides a welcome break for the maintenance crews of the USAF's 28th Bombardment Wing, working on a Boeing B-29A dispersed around the airfield perimeter at Scampton during the summer of 1948.***
Brig Gen Brian S Gunderson USAF Retd

Left: **Gliding for the cadets of the Air Training Corps has been a long-standing activity within the county and Slingsby Cadet TX.1 TS336 of 22 Gliding School is seen here at Grimsby (Waltham) in 1950.** *P H T Green*

Above left: **The first North American Harvards had entered service with the RAF at Spitalgate in January 1939. When this KF-serialled example was photographed in 1950, it was being operated by the RAF College, Cranwell. Note the four-letter code sequence – a system used by Training and Reserve Command aircraft between 1946 and 1951.** *RAF Cranwell*

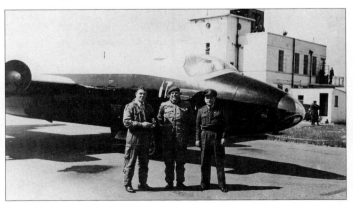

Above right: **Binbrook was destined to receive the RAF's first Canberra B.2 on 25th May 1951, when Wg Cdr R P Beamont, English Electric Company's Chief Test Pilot, delivered WD936 for use by 101 Squadron. Also in the picture are the Station Commander, Group Captain W Sheen (centre), and Wing Commander H P Connolly (right), Wing Commander Flying.** *P H T Green collection*

Above: A key unit to operate from Manby was the RAF Handling Squadron, the unit which wrote the 'Pilot's Notes' for all new aircraft to enter military service. The variety of the task is clearly visible in this formation which was flown from Manby on 24th September 1953. Types shown include the Athena T.2, Sea Prince, Marathon T.1, Wyvern TF.4, Sea Hawk, Attacker, Vampire T.11, Meteor NF.11, and Canberra B.2. MoD

Right: Another aircraft to first enter RAF service in Lincolnshire was the Vickers Varsity T.1. It served with 201 Advanced Flying School at Swinderby from late 1951, replacing another ageing Vickers type, the Wellington. One of the first deliveries was WF330, which is seen here airborne from Swinderby in October 1951.
P H T Green collection

Canberra B.6s of 109 and 139 Squadrons from Hemswell, seen in formation over the Lincolnshire coast, south of Cleethorpes, in May 1955. Flight

The RAF Flying College at Manby used Strubby as a satellite airfield, and Handley Page Hastings WJ327 is seen here parked on one of Strubby's dispersals.
N Jackson via P Pountney

*Above: **Pleasure flying from Lincolnshire's holiday resorts was a regular feature of the summer months, both before and after the Second World War. Two of Norfolk Airways' Auster V aircraft (G-AMSZ in the foreground) were operating from the beach at Cleethorpes in June 1955.** P H T Green*

*Right: **During 1954 the A V Roe works at Bracebridge Heath refurbished Avro 504 D7560 for display in the Science Museum. The aircraft is shown here with the band of workers involved in the work before it was returned to London for display.** P H T Green collection*

A V Roe's works at Bracebridge Heath handled the repair of many aircraft, but its lack of an airfield in later years necessitated that aircraft be towed along the A15 to nearby Waddington for flight-testing. Here an Avro Anson makes the somewhat ungainly journey in August 1955. Note that the road signs were hinged to allow clearance for the wings. *Lincolnshire Echo*

One of a number of Lincolnshire airfields to be allocated for use by the USAF in the mid-1950s, Sturgate was a deployment base for F-84F Thunderjets of the 27th Strategic Fighter Wing, from Bergstrom AFB, Texas, between May and August 1955. *Ron Brittain*

XA900 was one of the first Vulcan B.1s to arrive for 230 Operational Conversion Unit. It is shown here taxying in at Waddington on 25th March 1957. The Lincoln Coat of Arms motif displayed on the fin of this and other aircraft at RAF Waddington, reflects the close association of the RAF station with the City . *P H T Green collection*

One of Cranwell's de Havilland Vampire T.11 two-seat training aircraft, seen here in the late 1950s, has the aircraft serial number superimposed on the distinctive two-tone blue band marking of the RAF College. *Arthur Pearcy*

Lancaster B.I R5868, which began its service life at RAF Scampton with 83 Squadron, later moved to 467 Squadron at Waddington, and altogether completed 137 operations. After a period of storage it was returned to Scampton in March 1959 and took up 'gate guard' duties at the main entrance later that year, initially in the markings of 467 Squadron – as seen here – but later it carried 83 Squadron's code letters 'OL-Q'. It was removed from the gate in November 1970. After restoration work by 71MU at RAF Bicester, it went on display at the Royal Air Force Museum at Hendon on 12th March 1972, where it can still be seen today. *RAF Scampton*

Renowned for the fleet of Auster aircraft it used for pleasure flying during the summer months, part of the Skegness Air Taxi Service fleet is seen here at Skegness Aerodrome in the summer of 1964. D Stennett

For several years the College of Air Warfare operated its own aerobatic team, 'The Macaws', shown here making a formation approach to RAF Manby in the late 1960s. P H T Green collection

Gloster Meteors operated in Lincolnshire for many years, and F.8 WH291 of 85 Squadron was photographed in the Binbrook area in May 1969, whilst being flown by Flt Lt Peter Woodham, the Squadron's display pilot. RAF Binbrook

For a few years, Hemswell was the home of a number of light aircraft, including a home-built Luton Minor G-ATFW built by George Shield. It was photographed at Hemswell in November 1971. Note the home-made three-bladed propellor. P H T Green collection

Any suitable field can provide a temporary base for crop spraying aircraft, and Piper Pawnee G-AVDZ of Lincs Aerial Spraying was making use of a field at Croft Bank, near Skegness, for top-dressing operations during April 1974. W J Taylor

Development of the disused bomber base at Kirmington was carried out by Lindsey County Council and it is now known as Humberside Airport. Construction of a new terminal building is seen nearing completion in November 1973. The official opening took place on 26th March 1974, a few weeks before the boundary changes.
Grimsby Evening Telegraph

The rapid expansion of the North Sea oil and gas industry saw the development of a heliport at Strubby for use by oil and gas support helicopters. Sikorsky S-58T G-BCWD was part of Management Aviation's fleet and is shown parked at the heliport in October 1975. *W J Taylor*

Above: Coningsby was selected as the main training and operating base for the RAF's Phantom FGR.2 force, of which XV425/R and XV400/I of 29 Squadron, which had reformed on 1st January 1975, were typical. W J Taylor

Right: Visiting Skegness Aerodrome on 7th August 1988, Bulldog T.1 XX520 of the Central Flying School, RAF Scampton, was being used as a runabout to deliver the commentator for a display over the sea-front by the RAF Aerobatic Team, 'the Red Arrows'. W J Taylor

Below: Binbrook and the Lightning are synonymous, and F.3 XR749 is seen here in November 1985 sporting a huge rendition of the station's lion emblem, plus dark blue spine and fin on its otherwise two-tone grey colour scheme. MCP

Above: Aerial Spraying was carried out extensively in the county during the 1960s and 1970s, but due to environmental pressure it declined during the 1980s and is now virtually non-existant. Piper Pawnee and Grumman Ag Cat were the main types used. Ag Cat G-BDZF of Miller Aerial Spraying Limited is seen at its home base of Wickenby on 22nd July 1976. P H T Green

With the demise of the Lightning force at Binbrook, several aircraft underwent a lingering death as decoys and battle damage repair training aids. Some aircraft then went on to be used for crash/rescue training, such as 8808M/XP695 (rear), prior to being scrapped. *W J Taylor collection*

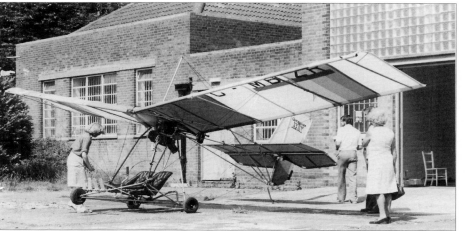

Microlight aircraft have been a relatively recent addition to the county's aviation scene, and an Eipper Quicksilver MXII is seen here being prepared for flight at Manby in July 1982. *W J Taylor*

Normally the Bloodhound missiles of D Flight, 85 Squadron, Barkston Heath, would have pointed skywards. However, when this photograph was taken on 1st July 1990, the Bloodhound unit had just been withdrawn from its operational declaration, prior to removal of the missiles and closure of the site. Subsequently, the missile site at Barkston Heath went on to be used by the Department of Initial Officer Training at Cranwell as a practical training area. *W J Taylor collection*

Aerial crop spraying remains a limited summer activity in the county and Piper Pawnee G-BFBW is seen here reloading at a farm airstrip at Ropsley Heath, near Grantham, on 17th July 1990. *W J Taylor*

Left: *The air defence variant of the Tornado was introduced into RAF service with 229 OCU at Coningsby in November 1984. Tornado F.2 ZD935 is seen preparing for a sortie from there in June 1986, only a month before they began to be superseded by the improved F.3s. The F.3s continue in service at Coningsby with Nos 5, 29 and 56 (Reserve) Squadron – the latter having taken over the role of the OCU from another 'shadow' unit, 65 Squadron, during 1993.* W J Taylor

Centre left: *Waddington is nowadays the home of 8 Squadron and the Royal Air Force fleet of Boeing E-3D Sentry AEW.1 aircraft. These aircraft have seen service in the Gulf and Bosnia in addition to monitoring Britain's air space.* MAP

Bottom left: *Many of the Pawnee crop spraying aircraft have seen a new lease of life as glider tugs. Here G-BDWL receives attention at the Peterborough and Spalding Gliding Club at Crowland, before commencing tugging operations on 22nd May 1993. The glider is Slingsby Dart BGA1975.* W J Taylor

Bottom right: *Having closed as an RAF station on 18th December 1990, North Coates has seen a new lease of life as a base for light aircraft, a number of which arrived for a fly-in, held on 5th September 1993.* P H T Green